Table of Contents

	Page
Section 1: Introduction	**2**
Preface	2
Key Contacts	3
Section 2: My Life's Journey Love Letter	**4**
Favorite Relationships	5
Other Favorites	5
Beliefs and Values	6
Life Lessons Learned	6
Life's Themes	7
Section 3: My Aspirations Love Letter	**8**
General Aspirations	8
Aspirations for My Family	9
Aspirations for Specific Loved Ones	10
Aspirations for Others	12
Aspirations for My Care While Living	14
Upon My Death	19
Section 4: My Special Causes Love Letter	**21**
The Organizations and Causes I Care About	22
Special Causes Documents	24
Section 5: My Guidance Love Letter	**25**
Personal, Health, Financial, and Estate Affairs	26
Legal Affairs, Documents, & Other Notices	40
Section 6: Appendices	**43**
Suggestions for Completing and Sharing Your Love Letters	43
About The Aspirational Philanthropist Learning Series℠	46
About the Author & Publisher	47

Copyright © 2022 Aspire to Give, LLC   www.AspiretoGive.com

Section 1: Introduction

"This brief lifetime is my opportunity to receive love, deepen love, grow in love, and give love."

- Henri Nouwen

Dear_____,

As a reflection of my enduring love, there are four sets of "love letters" within this journal. These love letters reflect my life's journey, my deepest aspirations and philanthropic causes, and a guide to my personal, health, financial, and estate affairs.

These love letters are non-legal supplements to my signed and binding legal documents. The love letters' purpose is to convey and clarify the significance and impact of my life as well as my intentions. Thus, I would like each family member, executor, trustee, guardian, and advisor to honor these love letters as a thoughtful and caring gift of love to my family.

Our life's journey is an ever-unfolding experience of growth, change, and transition during which we learn to live, love, and light the way for others. I hope that these love letters will ease this transition and light the way for you to pursue your hopes, dreams, and deepest aspirations.

To begin, you may want to review the table of contents and the suggestions in the appendix to understand the journal's layout and entries. Some love letter entries may point you to locations or others for access or additional guidance.

Please know that I love you dearly.

Love,

_____   _____
Name   Date

Copyright © 2022 Aspire to Give, LLC   www.AspiretoGive.com

In the event of my death or a severe health condition, please contact the following:

My primary point of contact (family member or friend)

Name: _____

Phone(s): _____ Email: _____

My secondary point of contact (family member or friend)

Name: _____

Phone(s): _____ Email: _____

Primary Professional Advisor:

Name: _____

Phone(s): _____ Email: _____

Website: _____

Other Key Persons to Notify:

Name: _____ Relationship: _____

Phone(s): _____ Email: _____

Name: _____ Relationship: _____

Phone(s): _____ Email: _____

Name: _____ Relationship: _____

Phone(s): _____ Email: _____

Name: _____ Relationship: _____

Phone(s): _____ Email: _____

Copyright © 2022 Aspire to Give, LLC   www.AspiretoGive.com

Section 2: My Life's Journey Love Letter

"The meaning of life is to find your gift. The purpose of life is to give it away."
- Pablo Picasso

Dear_____,

As a gift of love, sharing my life's journey is my way of conveying to you my relationships, themes, beliefs, values, and lessons learned over my lifetime. Please consider this shared wisdom to pursue your hopes, dreams, and aspirations. I hope that you may learn from my journey and that it will provide you comfort and guidance.

Love,

_____

Favorite Relationships
(Examples: spiritual, family, friends, teachers, mentors, coaches, teammates)

_____

_____

_____

_____

_____

_____

_____

_____

Other Favorites
(Examples: hobbies, books, memories, vacations, accomplishments, music, food)

_____

_____

_____

_____

_____

_____

_____

Copyright © 2022 Aspire to Give, LLC						www.AspiretoGive.com

Beliefs and Values

(Examples: spiritual, ethics, family, relationships, work ethic, altruism, kindness)

_____
_____
_____
_____
_____
_____
_____

Life Lessons Learned

(Examples: relationships, career, business, family, hobbies, personal, sports)

_____
_____
_____
_____
_____
_____
_____
_____

Copyright © 2022 Aspire to Give, LLC   www.AspiretoGive.com

Life's Themes

(Examples: faith, family, friends, life-long learning, sharing, teaching, giving)

_____
_____
_____
_____
_____
_____
_____
_____
_____
_____
_____
_____
_____
_____
_____
_____
_____
_____
_____

Section 3: My Aspirations Love Letter

"The future belongs to those who believe in the beauty of their dreams."
- Eleanor Roosevelt

General Aspirations

(Please circle what you **agree** with.)

- I would like my family members and friends to celebrate my life, remember, learn the lessons from my life, and share funny, uplifting stories.
- I would like to be forgiven for the times I have hurt my family, friends, and others.
- I would like others to know that I forgive them.
- I would like for my family members and loved ones to know that because of the faith that I have, I do not fear death itself.
- I think it is not the end but a new beginning for me.
- As necessary, I would like family members to make peace with each other.
- I would like others to look at my death as a time of personal growth.
- I would like others to get counseling if they have trouble with my death.

Copyright © 2022 Aspire to Give, LLC   www.AspiretoGive.com

- I want others to celebrate my life and learn from my life's journey.
- If anyone asks how I want to be remembered, please say the following about me.

  _____
  _____
  _____

- Other general aspirations:

  _____
  _____
  _____

Aspirations for My Family

The following are wishes, wants, and hopes for my family.

1. _____
   _____
   _____
   _____

2. _____
   _____
   _____
   _____

3. _____
   _____
   _____
   _____

Copyright © 2022 Aspire to Give, LLC　　　　　　　　www.AspiretoGive.com

Aspirations for Specific Loved Ones

The following are my hopes and dreams for specific loved ones. Please insert name and your aspirations. If a specific aspirational letter is written for each loved one, state its location and access.

1. _____-_____
   _____
   _____
   _____
   _____
   _____

2. _____-_____
   _____
   _____
   _____
   _____

3. _____-_____
   _____
   _____
   _____
   _____

Copyright © 2022 Aspire to Give, LLC   www.AspiretoGive.com

4. _____-_____

_____

_____

_____

_____

_____

5. _____-_____

_____

_____

_____

_____

_____

6. _____-_____

_____

_____

_____

_____

_____

Copyright © 2022 Aspire to Give, LLC   www.AspiretoGive.com

Aspirations for Others

Listed below are my aspirations for dear friends or others who are important to me.

1. _____-_____

   _____

   _____

   _____

   _____

   _____

2. _____-_____

   _____

   _____

   _____

   _____

   _____

3. _____-_____

   _____

   _____

   _____

   _____

Copyright © 2022 Aspire to Give, LLC   www.AspiretoGive.com

4. _____-_____
   _____
   _____

5. _____-_____
   _____
   _____

6. _____-_____
   _____
   _____

These aspirations are not intended to replace my will or other legacy planning documents signed by me. However, I express the desire that each family member, Executor, Trustee, and Guardian will honor these aspirations as a supplement to my legal documents and a true expression of my wishes and gift of love to my family.

_____   _____   _____
          Signature   Print Name   Date

Copyright © 2022 Aspire to Give, LLC			www.AspiretoGive.com

Aspirations for My Care While Living

Aspirations for Medical Treatment

I believe that my life is precious, and I deserve to be treated with dignity. When the time comes that I am very sick and am not able to speak for myself, I would like to let my family, my doctors, other health care providers, my friends, and all others know the kind of medical treatment that I want or don't want by my Advanced Medical Directive. My aspirations below serve to clarify my intent that might not be explicitly stated in my medical directive.

A.   General Aspirations (Circle those bullets you agree with or add additional guidance.)

- I do not want to be in pain. I want my doctor to give me enough medicine to relieve my pain, even if that means I will be drowsy or sleep more than otherwise.

- I do not want anything done or omitted by my doctors or nurses *to take my life*. I want to be offered food and fluids by mouth and kept clean and warm.

- To reduce the burden on my loved ones and assure dear friends and relatives know of my condition, I ask that my medical condition be routinely updated on a website such as caringbridge.org or a similar website by a close loved one.

- Other requests:

  _____

  _____

  _____

B.   If I am close to death:

If my doctor and another health care professional both decide that I am likely to die within a short period, and life-support treatment would only postpone the moment of my death (**circle one of the following**):

- I want to have life-support treatment.

- I want to have life-support treatment if my doctor believes it could help, but I want my doctor to stop giving me life-support treatment if it is not helping my health condition or symptoms.

- I do not want life-support treatment. If it has been started, I want it stopped.

- Other requests:

_____

_____

C.   **If I am in a coma and not expected to wake up or recover:** If my doctor and another health care professional both decide that I am in a coma from which I am not likely to wake up or heal or I have brain damage, and life-support treatment would only postpone the moment of my death (**circle <u>one</u> of the following**):

- I want to have life-support treatment.

- I want to have life-support treatment if my doctor believes it would be helpful, but I want my doctor to stop giving me life-support treatment if it is not helping my health condition or symptoms.

- I do not want life-support treatment. If it has been started, I want it stopped.

- Other requests:

_____

_____

Copyright © 2022 Aspire to Give, LLC   www.AspiretoGive.com

D. **If I have permanent and severe brain damage and I am not expected to recover:** If my doctor and another health care professional both decide that I have permanent and severe brain damage (for example, I can open my eyes, I cannot speak or understand) and I am not expected to recover, and life-support treatment would only postpone the moment of my death
(**circle one of the following**):

- I want to have life-support treatment.

- I want to have life-support treatment if my doctor believes it would be helpful, but I want my doctor to stop giving me life-support treatment if it is not helping my health condition or symptoms.

- I do not want life-support treatment. If it has been started, I want it stopped.

- Other requests:

_____
_____
_____

E. **If I am in another condition under which I do not wish to be kept alive:**

I list below if there is another condition for which I do not wish to have life-support treatment. In this condition, I believe that the costs and burdens of life-support treatment are too much and not worth the benefits to me. Therefore, in this condition, I do not want life-support treatment. (Please write the disease or conditions in the space below, or leave the space blank if you have none):

_____
_____
_____

Copyright © 2022 Aspire to Give, LLC   www.AspiretoGive.com

Aspirations For My Comfort

(Please circle what you agree with and, as necessary, add you own aspirations for your comfort.)

- If possible, I prefer to be treated at my home.

- I do not want to be in pain. I want my doctor to give me enough medicine to relieve my pain, even if that means I will be drowsy or sleep more than otherwise.

- If I show signs of depression, nausea, shortness of breath, or hallucinations, I want my caregivers to do whatever they can to help me.

- I would like to have a relaxed, moist cloth put on my head if I have a fever. I want my lips and mouth kept moist to stop dryness.

- I would like to have warm baths often. I wish to be kept fresh and clean at all times.

- I would like to be massaged with warm oils as often as possible.

- I would like to have my favorite music played, which is: _____

_____

_____

- I would like to have personal care like shaving, nail clipping, hair brushing, and teeth brushing, as long as they do not cause me pain or discomfort.

- I would like to have religious readings, well-loved poems, and stories read aloud to include the following:

_____

_____

- Other requests for my comfort:

_____

Copyright © 2022 Aspire to Give, LLC   www.AspiretoGive.com

Aspirations for My Care

(Please circle what you **agree** with.)

- I would like to have people with me when possible. I want someone to be with me when it seems that death is imminent.

- I would like to have my hand held and be talked to when possible, even if I don't seem to respond to the voice or touch of others.

- I would like to have others praying for me when possible.

- I would like to have the members of my place of worship notified that I am sick and asked to pray for me.

- For visitation, I prefer that that family and friends (circle all that apply):
    - Check with my caregiver/family contact
    - Check for updates on CaringBridge
    - Visit me
    - Not visit me

- I would like to be cared for with kindness and cheerfulness, not sadness.

- I would like to have pictures of my loved ones in my room, near my bed.

- I would like to die at home if that can be arranged.

- Other requests for my care: _____

_____

_____

Upon My Death

I am an organ donor (check/circle one): ☐ Yes ☐ No

My wish (check/circle one): ☐ Cremation ☐ Burial

The following loved one knows my funeral plans: _____

- Obituary written: ☐ Yes ☐ No   If yes, location: _____

Share obituary or notice of death (check/circle all that apply):

☐ Place of worship ☐ Printed Newspaper ☐ Funeral Home Website ☐ Social Media

☐ College(s) _____ ☐ Employer(s): _____

☐ Other: _____

Obituary newspaper locations (cities): _____

Funeral Home: _____

Phone: _____

Cemetery/ Columbarium: _____

Plot/Drawer # _____

Prepaid burial/cremation costs? ☐ Yes ☐ No Comments: _____

If cremation, disposal of ashes: _____
_____

- If Burial (check/circle all that apply):

☐ Open casket ☐ Embalming

☐ Mementos in casket: _____

☐ Clothes to be worn for burial: _____

☐ Other requests: _____

- Funeral home choices (example: casket, tombstone, vault)

    Quality: ☐ High ☐ Medium ☐ Low

    Expense: ☐ High ☐ Medium ☐ Least

Comments on funeral home choices: _____
_____

Type of service (check/circle all that apply):

☐ Place of Worship ☐ Graveside ☐ Memorial ☐ Celebratory ☐ No Service ☐ Other
_____
_____

If there is a memorial service, I would like to include the following (list music, songs, readings, pictures, or other specific requests that you have):
_____
_____
_____
_____
_____

Other requests: _____
_____
_____

Preferred Officiant to Perform Service: _____

Pallbearers: _____
_____
_____

Additional Notes: _____
_____
_____

Obituary Reading(s):
_____
_____
_____

Tombstone/Columbarium Engraving: _____
_____

Charitable Donations at My Death:
_____
_____

In lieu of flowers, please ask for donations to: _____
_____
_____

Other special requests:
_____

Section 4: My Special Causes Love Letter

"Life's most persistent and urgent question is, What are you doing for others?"
- Martin Luther King, Jr.

Dear_____

This love letter shares the special philanthropic causes that have been instrumental and inspirational in my life. It clarifies my intent and dedication to these important causes and organizations that align with my values and passions. It is in giving that we receive. The sharing of our gifts brings us happiness and meaning and makes an impact. I encourage each of you to take quiet time to reflect on special causes meaningful to you and give your unique gifts to improve the human condition for future generations.

Love,

_____

The Organizations and Causes I Care About

These special causes and organizations have been inspirational in my life. After each of the listed causes, I share why and how they have inspired me.

1. _____

   _____
   _____
   _____
   _____

2. _____

   _____
   _____
   _____
   _____

3. _____

   _____
   _____
   _____
   _____

4. _____

_____
_____
_____
_____

5. _____

_____
_____
_____
_____

6. _____

_____
_____
_____
_____

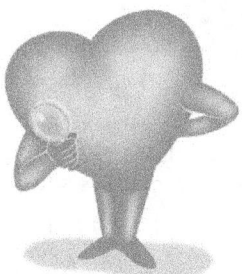

Special Causes and Organizational Documents

Please check/circle the applicable documents and add their location, access, and notes.

- ☐ Charitable trust: _____
- ☐ Donor-advised fund: _____
- ☐ Private foundation: _____
- ☐ Keepsake(s) instructions: _____
- ☐ Legacy Endowment Fund: _____
- ☐ Nonprofit Pledge(s): _____
- ☐ Church Pledge: _____
- ☐ Donor Letter of Intent: _____
- ☐ Bequest (will or trust): _____
- ☐ Nonprofit naming rights (program, room, etc.): _____
- ☐ Tangible Property: _____
- ☐ Other: _____
- ☐ Other: _____
- ☐ Other: _____

Organization #1: _____   Contact Name: _____

Phone(s): _____   Email: _____

Website: _____   Other Info: _____

Organization #2: _____   Contact Name: _____

Phone(s): _____   Email: _____

Website: _____   Other Info: _____

Organization #3: _____   Contact Name: _____

Phone(s): _____   Email: _____

Website: _____   Other Info: _____

Section 5: My Guidance Love Letter

"To have his path made clear for him is the aspiration of every human being in our beclouded and tempestuous existence."

- Joseph Conrad, The Mirror of the Sea (1906)

Dear _____,

This love letter includes what you should know regarding my personal, financial, health, and legal affairs. While seemingly practical and rational, these documents and guidance are gifts of love to you to reduce stress, save you time, and simplify access, administration, and estate settlement.

Love,

_____

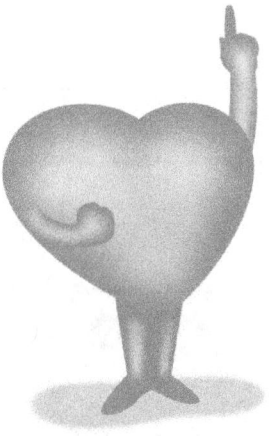

Personal, Health, Financial, and Legal Affairs

Assets

My investments, banking, real estate, and other properties are listed below. Please refer to the "My Digital, Social Media, and Online Legacy" section of this love letter to locate and access online usernames and passwords.

Investment Account #1:

Institution: _____

Account Number: _____ Account Type: _____ Ownership: _____

Phone(s): _____

Email: _____

Website: _____

Investment Account #2:

Name: _____

Account Number: _____ Account Type: _____ Ownership: _____

Phone(s): _____

Email: _____

Website: _____

Investment Account #3:

Name: _____

Account Number: _____ Account Type: _____ Ownership: _____

Phone(s): _____

Email: _____

Website: _____

Investment Account #4:

Name: _____

Account Number: _____ Account Type: _____ Ownership: _____

Phone(s): _____

Email: _____

Website: _____

Bank or Credit Union #1:

Name: _____

Account Number: _____ Account Type: _____ Ownership: _____

Email: _____

Website: _____

Copyright © 2022 Aspire to Give, LLC   www.AspiretoGive.com

Bank or Credit Union #2:

Name: _____

Account Number: _____ Account Type: _____ Ownership: _____

Phone(s): _____

Email: _____

Website:_____

Employer:

Name: _____

Benefits: _____

Employer Retirement Plan: Type: _____ Plan Custodian: _____

Phone(s): _____

Email: _____

Website:_____

Mortgage Holder:

Institution: _____

Phone(s): _____

Email: _____

Website:_____

Copyright © 2022 Aspire to Give, LLC   www.AspiretoGive.com

Property Insurance:

Institution: _____

Phone(s): _____

Email: _____

Website: _____

College Savings Accounts: **Number of Accounts:** _____

Institution: _____

Phone(s): _____

Email: _____

Website: _____

Statement Location: _____

Phone: _____

Personal Home: _____

Titled as: _____

Approx. $ Value: _____

Approx. $ Loan Outstanding: _____

Mortgage Holder: _____

Phone: _____

Statement Location: _____

Copyright © 2022 Aspire to Give, LLC   www.AspiretoGive.com

Other Real Estate: _____

Titled as: _____

Approx. $ Value: _____

Approx. $ Loan Outstanding: _____

Mortgage Holder: _____

Phone: _____

Statement Location: _____

Other Real Estate: _____

Titled as: _____

Approx. $ Value: _____

Approx. $ Loan Outstanding: _____

Mortgage Holder: _____

Phone: _____

Statement Location: _____

Other Property (e.g., collectibles):

Contact: _____

Guidance on disposition: _____

Phone: _____

Statement Location: _____

Money is owed by:

Name: _____

Address: _____

Phone(s): _____

Email: _____

Amount: _____

Business Contracts: _____

_____

_____

_____

Intellectual Property: _____

_____

_____

_____

Other: _____

_____

_____

_____

Copyright © 2022 Aspire to Give, LLC   www.AspiretoGive.com

Non-Mortgaged Debt (e.g., credit cards, etc.)

Here is a list of our non-mortgage debt, including the contact's name and phone number and the location of any related documents.

Debt #1 Type: _____

Account Number: _____

Website: _____

Phone: _____

Debt Amount: _____

Statement Location: _____

Debt #2 Type_____

Account Number: _____

Website: _____

Phone: _____

Debt Amount: _____

Statement Location: _____

Debt #3 Type: _____

Account Number: _____

Website: _____

Phone: _____

Debt Amount: _____

Statement Location: _____

Comments on Non-Mortgaged Debt: _____

_____

Copyright © 2022 Aspire to Give, LLC   www.AspiretoGive.com

My Digital, Social Media, and Online Estate

Social Media (circle all that apply)   Facebook Y   N   Instagram Y   N

LinkedIn Y   N   Twitter   Y   N   WhatsApp Y   N   YouTube Y   N   Google Y   N

Other Social Media: _____

Username & Passwords Location: _____

Special Instructions: _____

Insurance

I have the following **life insurance** policies:

Type / Company / Policy # / Owner / Beneficiary(ies) / Death Benefit / Cash Value

_____

_____

_____

_____

_____

These policies can be found at: _____

I have the following **disability insurance** policies:

Company	Policy #	Policy Located At:
_____	_____	_____
Company	Policy #	Policy Located At:
_____	_____	_____

Copyright © 2022 Aspire to Give, LLC   www.AspiretoGive.com

I have the following **long term care** insurance policies:

Company   Policy #   Policy Located At:
_____   _____   _____

I have the following **health insurance** policies (including Medicare, Dental, Vision, and Supplemental Policies):

Company   Policy #   Policy Located At:
_____   _____   _____

Company   Policy #   Policy Located At:
_____   _____   _____

Company   Policy #   Policy Located At:
_____   _____   _____

_____

I have the following **other insurance** policies:

Type   /   Company   /   Policy #   /   Policy Location   /   Comments

Auto: _____

Umbrella:_____

Home: _____

Other: _____

Other: _____

- If disabled, please pay _____ do not pay _____ the premiums on the policies with family benefits.

- If disabled, my life policy allows ____ does not allow _____ prepayment of death benefits.

- If disabled, my life policy allows _____ does not let ____ you to stop making premium payments.

- If disabled, my disability policy allows ____ does not let _____ you stop making premium payments.

Employment

Company H/R Website: _____

Phone #: _____

Special Notes: _____

_____

_____

_____

_____

_____

Copyright © 2022 Aspire to Give, LLC   www.AspiretoGive.com

I have the following benefits where I worked (brief description):

- Retirement Plan(s) (circle):   Pension   Y   N   401k /457/ 403b   Y   N

    Retirement Plan Notes: _____

    _____

    _____

- Life Insurance:
    _____

- Health Insurance:
    _____

- Long Term Care Insurance:
    _____

- Disability Insurance:
    _____

- Deferred Compensation:
    _____

- Stock Ownership:
    _____

- Stock Options:
    _____

- Cafeteria Plan:
    _____

- Other:
    _____

    _____

I have appointed (in the above documents) the following persons to act on my behalf if I become disabled:

Financial Power of Attorney: 1st_____   2nd _____

Medical Power of Attorney: 1st_____2nd _____

I request _____ do not request _____ that the persons have the above powers of attorney act on my behalf rather than a guardian being appointed unless my family believes guardianship is necessary.

In the event of my incapacity, I do ____ do not ____ want to be kept home as long as possible, considering the cost.

I have ____ do not have ____ a divorce decree which may require that certain payments be made after I am disabled or after my death.

General Information

I do ____ do not ____ have a safety deposit box or personal safe. The code/combination key can be found: _____.

The safety deposit box or safe can be found at
_____.

Copyright © 2022 Aspire to Give, LLC   www.AspiretoGive.com

I am _____ am not_____ a military veteran. Branch: _____ Years of Service:_____

I have____ have not____attached a list of persons or organizations I want to receive my possessions when I die.

I may receive an inheritance from: _____

Upon my death, my heirs will____ will not ____ receive a distribution or benefits from a trust. If yes, the Trust was created by: _____.

The Trust documents can be found at:
_____
_____

I am ___am not ___currently the trustee of a trust. If a trustee, the trust document is located at:
_____
_____

I am____ am not____ a beneficiary of a trust. If so, the trust Document is located at:
_____
_____

My social security # is: _____

My state driver's license # is: _____

My passport # is: _____

The passport can be found: _____
_____

Copyright © 2022 Aspire to Give, LLC   www.AspiretoGive.com

I am ____ am not ____ entitled to military benefits. List the benefits:
_____
_____

I am____am not____entitled to other benefits. List the benefits:
_____
_____

Additional Notes:
_____
_____
_____
_____
_____
_____

Legal Affairs, Documents, & Other Notices

(Please check/circle all that apply and the location)

- ☐ Personal will — Location: _____
- ☐ Revocable trust — Location: _____
- ☐ Another trust (type): _____ — Location: _____
- ☐ Advanced medical directive (health) — Location: _____
- ☐ Living will — Location: _____
- ☐ Celebration of life, burial, cremation — Location: _____
- ☐ Other records (divorce, adoption, veterans) — Location: _____
- ☐ Organ donor designation (driver's license) — Location: _____
- ☐ Financial power of attorney — Location: _____
- ☐ Beneficiary forms (primary/contingent) — Location: _____
- ☐ Real estate titles — Location: _____
- ☐ Cars/boat titles — Location: _____
- ☐ Transfer on death (TOD) — Location: _____
- ☐ Payable on death (POD) — Location: _____
- ☐ Handwritten note to the family — Location: _____
- ☐ Handwritten notes to individual loved ones — Location: _____
- ☐ Note to special friend or beneficiary — Location: _____
- ☐ Letter of instructions & organization — Location: _____
- ☐ Digital /social media letter of instructions — Location: _____
- ☐ Revocable Living Trust — Location: _____
- ☐ Insurance Trust — Location: _____

Copyright © 2022 Aspire to Give, LLC   www.AspiretoGive.com

- ☐ Minor's Trust — Location: _____
- ☐ Custodial Account — Location: _____
- ☐ Do Not Resuscitate (DNR) — Location: _____
- ☐ Do Not Intubate (DNI) — Location: _____
- ☐ Pre-Nuptial Agreement — Location: _____
- ☐ Post-Nuptial Agreement — Location: _____
- ☐ Divorce Decree — Location: _____
- ☐ Citizenship Papers — Location: _____
- ☐ Veterans' Discharge (DD214) — Location: _____
- ☐ Retirement Plan Beneficiary — Location: _____
- ☐ Business Documents — Location: _____
- ☐ Business Notes:

_____

_____

_____

- ☐ Additional Notes:

_____

_____

_____

_____

_____

_____

Copyright © 2022 Aspire to Give, LLC   www.AspiretoGive.com

Estate Attorney:

Name: _____

Phone(s): _____

Email: _____

Website:_____

Business Attorney:

Name: _____

Phone(s): _____

Email: _____

Website:_____

Section 6: Appendices

Suggestions for Completing & Sharing Your Love Letters

"The journey of a thousand miles begins with one step."
- Lao Tzu

Completing these love letters may appear overwhelming! If you have lost a loved one, you understand the emotional stress, disruption, hassle, and uncertainty of a tragic loss. The purpose of these love letters is to ease the stress and reduce the trauma of loss during emotional life transitions such as severe health condition or death of a loved one.

Listed below are some suggestions and considerations to complete your love letters.

1. Before you begin, you may want to **survey each section's layout and the requested entries.** These are *your* love letters. Please edit, tailor, and complete *Love Letters to My Family* to meet your personal and family preference, circumstances, and needs. For example:
    a. Some love letter sections may appeal to you, and some may not.
    b. You may want to modify or add entries that are important to you.
    c. Some entries are simple, easy, and quick, yet others may require a conversation with your spouse or significant other, parent, or adult child.

2. **Before you make any entries, you may want to share** *Family Love Letters to My Family* with a spouse, significant other, parent, adult child, or a dear friend. Let them thumb through the love letters and provide suggestions. Before sharing the journal, you may want to identify the most challenging entries and seek their input.

3. **To engage others and facilitate completion**, you may want to:
    (1) Identify those sections and entries that you might complete independently.
    (2) Assess the personalities of your loved ones. If you are not inclined to complete one or more sections of the love letters, another family member

may be more organized, see more value, or be willing to complete the love letters.

(3) Assess the age, health condition, willingness, and ability of the individual who may complete specific entries or sections of the love letters for you.

(4) In some cases, you may want to complete the love letters jointly with a loved one. In some cases, the love letters serve as a 3rd party reason to complete the entries together. Completing jointly with a loved one may also facilitate family sharing and bonding.

(5) In some cases (such as declining health), it may be necessary for a loved one to complete the entries on another's behalf.

(6) As a way to engage and facilitate important and meaningful conversations, consider *Love Letters to My Family* as a gift to a loved one.

4. **Recognize the emotional or practical nature of the content**. The *My Aspirations* section may be more emotionally challenging to complete than the sensible and rational *My Guidance* section. Hence, the approach to complete the entries in each section may be very different. For example, some entries for the *My Guidance* section may be completed in a single setting at the end of a calendar quarter when financial statements arrive. In contrast, *My Aspirations* may require meaningful conversations, solitude, reflection, and planning.

5. **Take it in small steps**. Completing these love letters is a process that takes time and is not a single event. Some entries may require meaningful conversations, deep thought, and solitude to complete. It may take weeks or months to complete all the love letters. It is recommended that you spend 15-20 minutes periodically to complete a section (such as the *My Guidance*) or a single entry such as an aspiration for a loved one.

6. **Consider the impact of change and the need to review** and update your love letters. As we each continue our life journey, our personal, financial, and family circumstances change over time. Hence, making the entries <u>in pencil</u> may make sense to facilitate changes to your love letters.

7. **Completing *My Aspirations*.** The *My Aspirations* love letter is often the most personal, emotionally challenging, and meaningful section. It usually takes time, personal reflection, and meaningful conversations to crystallize your feelings, thoughts, and completion. Before you make any entries, you may want to share this section with your significant other or spouse, dear friend, parent, or adult child. Sharing with others provides the following benefits:
    (a) You raise the topic to top-of-mind awareness of loved ones.
    (b) It may be an excellent way to start and engage in a meaningful conversation.
    (c) You gain their input on completing the love letters.
    (d) If it is too emotionally challenging for you to complete, offer (or you could ask) them to complete it on your behalf.
    (e) It provides the opportunity to engage in learning about a loved one's life and may serve as a vital component of the written obituary.
    (f) It serves as an opportunity to share, write, and record your stories as another gift of love. Recorded stories may serve as keepsakes for children and grandchildren.

8. **Consistency of Aspirations**: Should you convey financial and family aspirations, it is **vitally important to ensure your aspirations are specific and consistent with your legally binding legal and contractual agreements** such as insurance and IRA beneficiary forms, investment form, trust, will, and other agreements. Legal documents and contracts are legally binding and have precedence over aspirations ("wishes and wants"). Please collaborate and seek guidance from your professional advisors to assure your love letter aspirations and legal intentions are aligned and consistent.

The Aspirational Philanthropist Learning Series℠

The Aspirational Philanthropist Learning Series℠ is a first-of-its-kind learning program for everyday people that seek to grow through their generosity. Participants learn more about themselves, their loved ones, and how to give generously and effectively to their families and philanthropic causes.

The series is available as the *Aspirational Philanthropist Certificate Program*, an Auburn University online, self-paced learning program that is accompanied with the workbook tailored to the participant's personal, family, and financial circumstances. The four courses are:

1. Fundamentals – Learn the five keys to unlocking donor generosity.
2. Discovery – Reveal and align personal strengths, passions, and purpose.
3. Design – Draft a tailored giving strategy for family and special causes.
4. Legacy – Transform a life of success into lasting significance and impact.

There are also three (3) books as part of *The Aspirational Philanthropist Learning Series℠* that supplement the program.

- *The 5 Keys to Unlock Donor Generosity*
- *The Donor's Workbook*
- *Love Letters to My Family*

_____

Please visit www.AspiretoGive.com to learn more. We appreciate all those who have provided input into this series. If you would like to help others and have suggestions to improve Love Letters to My Family, please email: Greg@AspiretoGive.com.

The content included in The Aspirational Philanthropist Learning Series℠ including Love Letters to My Family is for informational and educational purposes only. It should not be construed as advice or recommendations. Please consult with your professional advisors with any specific questions.

About Greg Doepke

Greg Doepke is an author, founder of Aspire to Give® Academy, and the architect, author, and instructor of the *Aspirational Philanthropist Learning Series*℠ — an online educational program for everyday people growing through their generosity. He also served as the inaugural Philanthropist in Residence at Auburn University's Cary Center for the Advancement of Philanthropy and Nonprofit studies. He is a member of the International Association for Advisors in Philanthropy and served on its Board of Directors.

Greg is a West Point graduate with the vision to unleash the inherent need and potential of the individual to give generously for good. With over twenty years of credentialed expertise in financial, estate, legacy, and philanthropic planning, Greg helped numerous families through life transitions, such as the death of a loved one, retirement, and sudden wealth.

Greg is married to Suzette, the inspiration for Aspire, the symbol of the giving spirit. Suzette is a retired kindergarten teacher who shares her example of generosity, caring, and love for family and friends. Suzette and Greg have two loving daughters, seven thriving grandchildren, and live in Auburn, Alabama.

About William Summey

William Summey, Ph.D., has served as the primary editor for *The Aspirational Philanthropist Learning Series*. William is an adjunct instructor in the College of Theology & Christian Ministry at Belmont University. William began his work with philanthropy as managing editor of Paragon Road's *Legacy Arts* magazine and has worked for over 23 years in the publishing industry. William resides with his family in Nashville, Tennessee.

www.ingramcontent.com/pod-product-compliance
Lightning Source LLC
Chambersburg PA
CBHW080955220526
45465CB00008BA/3301